CHILD WELFARE LEAGUE OF AMERICA

CWLA

STANDARDS FOR GROUP HOME SERVICE FOR CHILDREN

Child Welfare League of America, Inc.
67 Irving Place, New York, N.Y. 10003

Copyright © 1978 by the Child Welfare League of America, Inc.

ALL RIGHTS RESERVED

Neither this book nor any part may be reproduced or transmitted in any form or by any means, electronic or mechanical, including photocopying, microfilming, and recording, or by any information storage and retrieval system, without permission in writing from the publisher.

CHILD WELFARE LEAGUE OF AMERICA

67 Irving Place, New York, New York 10003

Library of Congress Catalog Card Number: 77-92899

ISBN: 0-87868-171-X

Current printing (last digit)
10 9 8 7 6 5 4 3 2 1

PRINTED IN THE UNITED STATES OF AMERICA

ACKNOWLEDGMENTS

Development of these standards for group home service for children was greatly aided by the work of the Technical Advisory Committee, whose members were selected on the basis of their expertness and special interest in group home service. They represented affiliated agencies of the Child Welfare League of America, the U.S. Department of Health, Education and Welfare and the American Academy of Pediatrics.

Members of the committee were:

Warren Braucher, Child and Family Services of Connecticut, Hartford
Joseph M. Collins, New England Home for Little Wanderers, Boston
James W. Cotter, Hillside Children's Center, Rochester
Susan Delasala, New York State Board of Social Welfare, New York
Thomas Edwards, Sheltering Arms Children's Service, New York
Martin Gula, Office of Child Development, HEW, Washington, D.C.
Thayer Heath, Parsons Child and Family Center, Albany
Henry Kite, Josephine B. Baird Children's Center, Burlington
Dr. Elizabeth A. Lawder, Children's Aid Society of Pennsylvania, Philadelphia
Dr. S. Norman Sherry, Cambridge, Massachusetts (for American Academy of Pediatrics)
Mrs. Anne Ternbach, Jewish Child Care Association, New York
Joseph L. Taylor, Association of Jewish Children, Philadelphia

The consultant who prepared the preliminary draft indicating the areas to be covered in the standards for group home service was the executive of an affiliated agency whose program was group home care.

Consultant: Ernest Hirschbach, Summerhill Homes° Montreal
Staff: Gloria T. Chevers, Clara J. Swan

Committee on Standards 1976
Board of Directors, Child Welfare League of America

Chairman: Steven A. Minter, Cleveland
David L. Ball, Jr., Detroit
Mrs. Morgan Davis, Houston
Peter W. Forsythe, New York
Mrs. Alvin P. Gutman, Elkins Park, Pennsylvania
James L. Hicks, New York

°Affiliation at time of work on the standards.

The Most Rev. Joseph A. McNicholas, Springfield, Illinois
William Neville, Meridian, Mississippi
Mrs. Lawrence A. Schei, Sacramento
Mrs. John Stennis, Jackson
Mrs. D.B. Udall, Tucson
Homer D. Webb, Jr., Cleveland

CONTENTS

Foreword vii

Introduction 1

1. Group Home Service as a Child Welfare Service 5

2. Social Service in Group Home Care 11

3. Program for Care and Treatment 22

4. The Physical Structure of the Group Home 37

5. Staffing the Group Home 48

6. Organization and Administration of Agencies Providing Group Home Service 53

7. Community Planning and Organization for Group Home Service 75

Selected References 79

Index 81

v

Standards for Group Home Service for Children

FOREWORD

Setting standards and improving practice in all social services for children have been major functions of the Child Welfare League of America since its formation more than 60 years ago. The 1955 study of the League's function and program reaffirmed that

> "continued development of standards designed to be used as objectives or goals, based on tested knowledge and approved practice in the various fields of service, should be given high priority in the League's program."

Standards point up assumptions that need to be tested and offer clues for research to obtain the knowledge required to serve children better. As we come to know what the essentials are for healthy growth of all children, we must restate the responsibility of society that child welfare services discharge: to provide for the child who would otherwise lack the conditions and opportunities favorable to the development, use and enjoyment of his individual capacities.

In 1955, the League undertook to formulate a series of standards for child welfare services in light of what is known today about the development of children, and tested, effective ways of serving them.

Standards for Group Home Service for Children is the first completely new set of standards for a child welfare service to be developed by the League since 1968, when the Preliminary Statement on Social Work Service for Children in Their Own Homes was published. Since that time there have been revisions of many of the standards and some standards, notably those for adoption service, have been revised several times.

The preparation of these standards represents in some ways a departure from the usual way of developing and revising standards. A consultant, who was the executive director of an agency whose program was devoted to group homes, wrote a preliminary draft indicating the areas that he thought should be covered in standards for group homes. The preparation further involved the examination of current practices and the assumptions on which they are based; a survey of professional literature and standards developed by other groups, such as mental health and state welfare departments; and study of the most recent scientific findings of social work and related fields, such as child development, education, mental health, psychology, medicine, psychiatry, sociology, genetics and anthropology, as they affect child welfare practices.

The material was put into standards format and a technical advisory committee of experts in group home services met several times to assist in resolving issues in group home care.

Another innovation in the development of these standards was a meeting at each of eight CWLA regional conferences in the spring of 1976, presided over by a member of the Standards Committee of the Board of Directors of the Child Welfare League, to discuss issues in group home care and to obtain information from the field that could be used in the final preparation of the standards. Before final board approval as a policy statement of the Child Welfare League, a draft of these standards was reviewed by local and national agency representatives, including affiliated agencies with group home programs, state departments of welfare, and other organizations interested in this kind of care for children. The final draft took into account all these discussions and participation.

Use of standards

These standards are intended to be goals for continuous improvement of services to children. They represent practices considered to be most desirable in providing the social services the community offers to various agencies out of its concern for children. These are, therefore, standards for social welfare services for children regardless of auspices or setting.

The standards are directed to all concerned with improvement of services to children: the general public, citizen groups, public officials, legislators, and the various professional groups; those responsible for administration of services, board members and agency staffs; agencies whose functions include planning for and financing community service; state departments entrusted by law with functions relating to licensing or supervision of organizations serving children; and federations of agencies having requirements for membership involving judgments on the nature of the organization and the kind of service rendered.

Standards can stimulate improvement of services only as they bring about dissatisfaction with present practices, and conviction that change is desirable. They offer a base for examining and questioning practice and the premises from which it has been developed, and for evaluating the performance of child welfare agencies and the adequacy of existing services.

Standards are of use in planning, organization and administration of services, and in establishing state and local licensing requirements. They provide content for teaching and training in child welfare, in schools of social work, through inservice training and staff development programs, and in orientation of boards and volunteers. They can help to explain and justify expenditures, budget requests to federated fund-raising bodies, and appropriation requests to legislatures.

Finally, standards can promote understanding of how each service may more effectively meet needs of children, what it should be expected to do, and how it can be used. In that way, standards can help to gain greater public interest, understanding and support for adequate services, legislation and financing.

Periodic review of standards

The Child Welfare League of America periodically reviews all its statements of standards. No standards of practice can be considered final; in one sense, the moment they are issued, they are out of date. Standards must be subject to continuous review and revision, in view of the constantly growing knowledge about children, human behavior and human ills. Developments in social and medical sciences; evaluation of the effectiveness of current social work practices, policies and programs; and shifting patterns of social values and social organization should be conducive to change in child welfare practice.

Joseph H. Reid
Executive Director, CWLA

Standards for Group Home Service for Children

INTRODUCTION

Assistance to children and youths* who cannot live with their own or another family has led to expansion of specialized foster care services, notably group homes. Care of children in group homes is not new, but the expansion of group homes as a specialized service has been extremely rapid. Concurrent with this expansion, and presumably related, is the increasing number of adolescents in North America who live away from their families. Although this service was originally perceived as essentially for youths, the specialized use of group homes for school-age children has also expanded.

These standards apply to group home services provided through organized social agencies that are supported by voluntary contributions and allocation of tax funds.

Under various other auspices, group homes—including those operated by mental health and correctional departments or organizations—have served a variety of children who are not viewed as dependent or neglected. These are children with specialized needs or circumstances who can be served in group home programs with individualized services rather than in a large institutional setting.

Although issuance of *CWLA Standards for Group Home Service for Children* is timely, the standards reflect practices in a service where new developments and experiences are constantly occurring; it is essential to emphasize flexibility and openness of approach. There is,

---

*For convenience in reading, "children and youths" are usually referred to as "children" in this volume.

however, no question that group home service is appropriate on a selective basis, and that the service must ensure care, protection and treatment that promote the well-being of children.

0.1 Society's responsibility for children

Children whose parents are absent or unable to function as parents require protection. Because children are unable to care for themselves, society, through its organized agencies, must assume responsibility for their care and protection.

0.2 Group home in the continuum of child welfare services

In the continuum of child welfare services, the group home has characteristics of both foster family and institutional services and has the similar goal of promoting the well-being of children who cannot live with their own families.

Group home service for children is based upon assumptions and convictions about

• the dignity of the child as an individual, with the right to the kind of care that meets his needs regardless of sex, race, color, creed, national origin or social circumstances

• the responsibility of society for children, which requires accountability to the community of any agency to which specific responsibility to provide care and service to dependent children has been delegated

• the importance of preserving and strengthening the child's relationship with family members, where possible, to avoid placement, and the use of appropriate services when separation is necessary

• the importance of continuing the expansion and application of knowledge and skill in work with children and families

In small housing units in the community, the agency-owned-and-operated group home has emerged as a new form of group care, as well as the choice for certain children, particularly the adolescent group, and as a transition between institutional care and return to family life. When a combined group and family life experience can be helpful, the family group home may be used. It is usually owned or rented by a family that contracts with the agency to care for a small group of children.

0.3 The children in group homes

Group home service evolved to offer care and services for children and youth in need of foster care.

For the many youths who increasingly require care outside of a family setting, group home service meets their individual and developmental needs, as well as the needs of some younger children for whom other forms of foster care are, for specific reasons, inappropriate.

0.4 The nature of group home service

Group home service is designed to strengthen the children's relationship with peers and adults, and in community activities.

It offers a relationship with a small group of peers in a home-type setting where they live and are assisted by selected adults to handle the complexities of their relationships in the home and the community, and to cope with family, community and other environmental expectations.

0.5 Value of group home service

Group home service is most helpful for children who have the capacity and willingness to participate actively with others in the home and in the community in a way that strengthens their social skills and self-reliance.

0.6 Responsibility of the agency

The agency is responsible for seeing that the needs of children are met in group home service.

It is essential that an agency that operates or purchases group home service for a child exercise its responsibility so as to ensure that a plan for each child for use of the service
- offers experiences for growth and maturation
- assures the child's stability, security and continuity
- provides recognition of the worth and respect of the child as an individual
- provides opportunities for relationships with peers and adults in a way that fosters self-respect
- regularly assesses the value of the service to ensure the well-being of the child

1

GROUP HOME SERVICE AS A CHILD WELFARE SERVICE

Group home service as described in these standards is given under the auspices of a social agency to provide care and services for a small group of children who are unable to live in their own homes, and who can be assured of continuity in their living situation and a sense of belonging by residence in a home that exists solely for them.

The social agency or the administration of the group home that controls and/or manages the home determines the orientation and philosophy of the service, which governs admission and discharge, program and treatment.

1.1* Characteristics of group home care

Among the child welfare services that society provides for its children, group home care is one form of residential care.

The group home has a clear definition of its purpose, the kind of child it can benefit, the number and age range of the children it serves. As a part of the community, the group home is indistinguishable from other family dwellings. The children use the same community services (school, recreation, religious participation, work opportunities, etc.) as children living in their own homes. Thus the children in care have the opportuni-

---

*Each standard is designated by a number, of which the digit preceding the decimal indicates the chapter in which it appears. The discussion following gives rationale, principles, implications, or steps in carrying out the practice.

ty to strengthen their ability to be fully participating members of the community in which they live.

They are assisted by adults who supervise and protect them, and guide them to greater social competence and self-confidence. (5.6)

Decisions about daily life, conduct, discipline and the atmosphere of the group home are made and carried out primarily by the group home staff in discussion with the children, within the boundaries of agency policy and the requirements of the service plan for each child. (3.1–3.11)

All staff members involved with the care and service for each child work together as a team to understand each other's goals and functions, to resolve disagreements, and to coordinate constructive efforts. There is a place for initiative and independent judgment within the team approach. (3.15–3.19)

1.2 Goals of group home service

The ultimate goal of group home service is the promotion of children's healthy development and the amelioration of individual problems that are personally or socially destructive.

Its immediate purpose is to enable children who lack necessary care to have a helpful environment that affords them an opportunity to
- limit the effect of social and emotional problems
- develop or strengthen constructive interpersonal relationships with adults and peers and with members of their families
- gain competence as individuals who participate constructively in educational, religious, interpersonal and other community activities, and thus achieve satisfaction from their daily living experiences

1.3 Conditions for choice of group home service

Group home service should be selected for children when adequate adjustment to family life is unlikely and the specialized services of a large facility are unnecessary.

Group home service can be appropriate for

- adolescents who have not lived away from their own homes before and find it difficult to adapt to foster families because of their own family ties or the behavioral problems that brought placement about; for many of these youths, life with a group of peers in a small home in the community is the preferred form of care
- schoolchildren who have had unsuccessful foster family placements, and who require a sense of continuity in one setting where their involvement in relationships can advance according to their needs
- children discharged from more intensive treatment institutional service, who need, at least for a time, a home life that is more structured and less intimate than typical family life
- children with behavioral patterns unacceptable to parents and foster parents, where the need is for strong professional support and guidance to participate appropriately in the life of the community
- children with physical, mental, and emotional difficulties who can meet the challenges of community life with the help of sufficient professional services and resources, including adequate staff to care for and protect them
- large sibling groups for whom the service plan is to keep the children together
- children who require diagnostic services, evaluative planning, emergency or crisis care. A group home used for this purpose is specialized to provide flexibility in service for children who need such care for a brief period. It offers protection as well as an opportunity for further planning for these children and their families. When such homes are located in or near the neighborhood of the children, it is easier to continue the child's usual community activities and relationships during an interim period. (1.5)

1.4 Children for whom group home service is inappropriate

Group home service should not be offered if it is not helpful to the children who require care.

Ordinarily, young children who must be separated from their parents should be with a substitute parental figure who can respond immediately to the care and distress of a limited number of children.

The protest and despair of young children that result in repeated foster home placements cannot be treated by placement in a group home.*

Some children require residential treatment or institutional care for their own protection and the protection of others: children who are severely aggressive or destructive to themselves and others who are inaccessible to intervention in their own homes or in the community.

Children with neurological or psychiatric disabilities will require a secure facility with special services.

1.5 Duration of services

The duration of group home services for each child should be based on his or her needs and the circumstances that require placement for care, protection or treatment.

Some examples include
- a brief period of care (1 to 2 months) for transitional planning, emergency care and protection of adolescents who are far from home, and for children with an immediate crisis in their family relationships, when intensive assessment of the children's needs and capacities is needed
- a planned period of care and social services for a child and family, directed toward reintegration of the family or the development of another stable life situation such as adoption, or legal guardianship with a responsible relative
- a period of specialized services for children with physical or emotional handicaps who are able to live in the community
- time-limited care for single pregnant young women and unmarried mothers designed to foster their capacity to handle ordinary life situations with competence on return to their own families or their own homes

---

*CWLA Standards for Foster Family Service 1.14.

- planned care for adolescents until they attain the legal status of adulthood in order to meet their continuing need for care and protection, when return to their own family is not possible and adoption or foster family service is not preferred by them or their families

1.6   Elements of group home service

Elements of service provided for or in behalf of the child should include the intake study and service to the parent.

The intake study comprises

- study and determination of service needed
- planning with the child, parents (legal guardian) or referring agency to determine a suitable plan for the child and family and to locate and help them use the community resources they need
- casework, groupwork and other related interventions necessary to foster the development and social functioning of the child and family
- evaluation of the service at periodic intervals to ascertain and respond to any changes in the needs of or service to the child and family. (2.7)

Service to the parent includes

- direct work with the parent (unless contraindicated) to strengthen and sustain the relationship of the family and child and to assist the parent with personal, family, and social problems that limit parental capability
- followup services to child and family when the child leaves the group home to ensure that the child is established or reintegrated into the family or into other living arrangements

1.7   Responsibility of a social agency that provides group home service

The social agency has the responsibility to ensure that comprehensive services are available to children in group homes.

This includes

• adequate knowledge of community resources to ensure that only those children who can use group home service are placed or remain in them

• linkage to a continuum of child welfare services for appropriate planning and assistance for the children who should not enter group homes

• administrative control of admission to a group home to ensure that no child is placed there because of expediency and that no child enters a group home unless the children in the residence can absorb the newcomer and the child can adjust to the particular group

2

SOCIAL SERVICE IN GROUP HOME CARE

Social work should be an integral part of group home care as a child welfare service. Social work skills are needed to preserve the parent/child relationship to the fullest extent possible for the child who is in group home care. Social work skills can assist a child and family to make the best use of the care and services of the group home program.

2.1 Need for social work

Social services should be available to children and their parents[*] to assist them with individual needs and family concerns.

Help and encouragement may be provided to

- decide whether group home care is the most satisfactory arrangement for the child and for the parents
- understand the possible effect on the child of separation from his family and of the group experience
- plan for and use the service
- carry parental responsibilities and deal with problems that affect the relationship of the parents to the child
- find other resources for the problem that made group home care necessary
- help the child directly (or through others) with social, emotional or health problems

To the group home staff the social worker contributes under-

---

*References to parents include legal guardians where applicable.

standing of the social factors in the child's life. The social worker contributes to the planning of a coordinated service.

The majority of families have problems for which help is needed to make use of social services and community resources. The parents may be faced also with practical difficulties, such as inadequate living arrangements, illness or conflict with the law, in meeting their child's needs. Some parents feel unprepared to care for their child or inadequate to do so.

The child will need help with separation from the family and the initial strains of living in an unfamiliar environment, conflicting standards of behavior, loss of neighborhood and school friends and activities. The child may have behavioral or emotional disturbances that require continual contact with the social worker, or treatment through prescribed daily living experiences in the group home or through referral to a mental health center or mental health personnel of the agency.

2.2 Use of service by other agencies

Interagency agreements should determine what services will be provided by the various agencies involved.

The agency that provides group home service should have written policies on offering its service, covering the kinds of case situation that may be referred, the children for whom the service is offered, its procedures, and the payment plan. Charges to the purchasing agency should be based on the full cost of service for the child. However, it should be clear whether the group home is offering a total service including social work planning for the child and family, or whether the agency placing the child retains responsibility for providing some services for the child and family.

2.3 Decisions about referrals

The agency that administers the group home service should make its decision about providing the service after discussion with the parents and child or the referring agency.

Use of group home service for a child by another agency should be considered first within the originating agency and then discussed with the group home agency.

The group home supervisor must determine whether the needs of the child can be met in the particular group home, based on the services available, the other children in the home, and the ability of the staff to meet the child's needs.

2.4 Referrals by the court

When children are committed to the agency by a court, a prompt intake study should serve as the basis for the agency to understand the child's needs and the care and protection required in order to provide service effectively.

Considerable skill, experience, and concern of the social worker about the individual and family problems of the parents and child will be needed to help the family collaborate in planning for and using the service, especially if a commitment is involuntary. Most often, parents will have mixed feelings about placement of the child; more anger and sadness occur when children are placed because of neglect or abuse than when the problem is abandonment or family dysfunction.

Grievance procedures should be provided for, both within the agency and the court. (6.13)

2.5 Application by child

The child who applies for himself should always be considered for service. For a preadolescent child parental consent should be obtained, wherever this is indicated.

2.6 Referrals from health and mental health residential facilities

When a referral is made on behalf of a child with special needs, such as a physical disability or emotional problem, the group home agency should be sure that all services required by the child are available and accessible to the child.

2.7 Intake study

Social work service should be responsible for making the intake study and for offering help throughout the intake process, including the ultimate decision to use the group home service or to make other plans.

> The agency referring a child for group home placement should furnish information about the need for the service, the family situation, pertinent developmental history, the child's relationships with parents, interests of the child, and the child's school progress, social relationships, and health.
>
> The social worker should inform the parents and the child about the service, including agency policies and practices, admission process, communication and contact between the child and family, need for and frequency of interviews with the social worker, the rights and responsibilities of the child, the family and the agency.
>
> The social worker should know the resources of the agency and the community in order to reach, with the family, a sound decision about the suitability of group home services as compared with other resources.

2.8 Referral to other agencies or resources

If it is determined that group home service is inadvisable, the social worker and the referring agency should assist the child and family to obtain more appropriate resources.

Initial Acceptance of Group Home Service

2.9 Setting goals for group home service

The social worker should reach an understanding with the parent and child about the specific goals for service to the child and family, after considering their circumstances and their capacity and motivation to deal with the problems and conditions in the social environment that could help or hinder progress.

Engaging in the development of mutual goals in relation to the individual situation, problem or need initiates a purposeful use of service by the child and family.

Goals should be realistically related to the individual situation, sufficiently limited and specific to encourage the parent and child to use and expand their capacities to deal with problems, yet flexible enough to allow for changes in the situation and in the use of the service.

2.10 Basis for continuing service

When a continuing service is to be given by the agency, the child and family should be helped to take part in discussing and understanding the resources and limitations of the situation in a way that gives evidence of the kind of help that will be offered, and establishes the basis for further service.

This involves explaining the specific services offered and the expectations for using them, the care provided, specific responsibilities and rights. In order to continue, some children and parents have to experience repeated explorations and discussions that demonstrate concern about them.

If the parents are to pay a fee, the arrangements should be a part of the intake process.

2.11 Continuing work with the parents

The parents and the child should have help in the preparation and admission of the child to the group home; and plans for direct help, or help through referral to other resources, on personal or environmental problems affecting relationships should be made with the parents.

The social worker should help the parent to understand and to explain clearly to a young child the reasons for placement, to help the child with the transition to the group home. Adolescents should take part in the discussion and decision about the use of the group home, the goal for service, and the preparation for admission.

In discussing the problems of the child, the social worker helps the parents to

- deal with feelings of anxiety, failure or anger in relation to the child's or their own difficulties, or the complexities that resulted in the decision for use of the service
- be regularly informed of the child's experiences in the group home and progress made
- deal with immediate practical problems that limit the family's functioning, particularly in child rearing. Referrals may be necessary for parents to obtain resources they need that are not provided by the agency.

Contacts with the family should be summarized for each conference about the child.

2.12 Direct work with the child

Social services provided to the child should be planned in collaboration with other staff who provide service and care for the child.

The social worker should have regular contacts with the child for counseling on problems in the group home, school, community activities, the family and, particularly for the older child, his or her future.

The social worker may use consultation with outside sources or refer the child for other services in the community.

2.13 Responsibility of the social worker in planning and evaluation

The social worker should be responsible for case management to assure a coordinated service in accordance with the treatment plan for the individual child.

- Each staff member and, when appropriate, consultants should participate in both planning for and evaluation of a child on the basis of their particular expertise.
- Whenever it becomes evident that the service is not helpful to the child, the social worker should help the parent (and when feasible, the child) make use of more appropriate resources.

2.14   Participation of the child in planning

Participation of the child and the way in which that participation will occur depend upon the child's age and maturity, the nature of the problem situation, and the helping method that has been selected.

> A child capable of taking some responsibility should be helped in appropriate ways to participate in planning for the service, as well as to participate actively in the service.
>
> This encouragement should be so offered as to reduce anxiety and increase the child's self-reliance and self-control. It is important for a child to experience the encouragement of the worker in learning to plan for his own needs.

Parental rights and responsibilities

2.15   Protection of parental rights

Parents should be protected in the exercise of their legal rights and responsibilities to their child unless there is evidence of their inability to carry out the parental role adequately, in which case society must intervene to protect the child. (6.15)

> Whether parents voluntarily decide to request placement for the child and want to use agency services, or whether the child is committed to the agency by court, the parents' rights and responsibilities must be respected. Concurrently, the parents should be informed that the agency must assume certain parental functions while the child receives care and treatment.
>
> When parents enter into a voluntary agreement with a child welfare agency for placement of their child, the rights and duties they retain and those they agree to delegate to the agency, and those the agency agrees to provide, should be fully agreed on by parents and agency. Such agreement should be in writing.
>
> Parents have the right to have the child returned on request (unless curtailed by law). If the agency decides that it is contrary to the child's best interests to agree to the parents' request, it must take proper legal action. Even after a court has

limited parental rights, short of terminating the parent-child relationship by judicial decree, the parents retain certain residual rights, including rights to a reasonable amount of contact and communication with the child, information about the child's whereabouts and condition, determination of religious affiliation, consent to adoption, inheritance and the right to notice of judicial proceedings involving the child. Responsibility for support usually follows.

If it is determined that the child's best interests can be served only if the parents' legal rights are limited or terminated through court action, the agency should discuss this with the parents and take the initiative in presenting such a recommendation to the court with a statement of the facts upon which it is based.

2.16 Responsibility for medical care

Responsibility for medical care should be delegated to the agency.

State law determines parental responsibility for the medical care of minors. The agency should obtain from the responsible parent consent for medical care and hospitalization. Parents should have the assurance that only in the event of an emergency will major surgery or hazardous treatment be authorized without prior consultation with them.

2.17 Responsibility to support

When parents are expected to pay for the cost of the child's care and service, payments should be assessed according to their ability to pay.

The parents who continue some financial support retain a responsibility that is often of considerable significance to the child.

Consideration should be given to the family's income and resources, their obligations and the needs of other members of the family.

2.18   Determination of religious affiliation

Parents have the right to designate the religious affiliation of the young child.
   The adolescent may choose his own religion.

2.19   Parents' contact with the child

Parents have a right to a reasonable number and frequency of visits with the child; regular contact between the parent and the child should be encouraged unless the plan for service excludes or limits a continuing relationship.
   Group homes should be near enough to the parents' home for the child and parents to visit regularly. If necessary, transportation for either the child or the parents, and time and place of visits, should be arranged flexibly.
   Brothers and sisters and other relatives should be encouraged to visit and to maintain a relationship with the child.
   Visits in the child's own family home should be less frequent than those in the group home or a neutral setting. They should be on a planned basis, such as part of the preparation for the return of the child to his own home.
   In the case of foster parents, their continuing role in terms of visiting and possible return of the child to the foster home should be clarified with them by the agency supervising them or by the agency caring for the child.
   Staff should observe the effect of parental visits on the child.
   Children and their parents may have to be helped together or individually to face the realities of the parents' problems and circumstances, and the difficulties that may arise for the child when seeing disturbed parents.

2.20   Written agreements

When a child is accepted for group home care, a written agreement between the parents and the agency should be prepared, signed by the parents, and by the social worker as the agency representative, and filed in the case record. A copy should be given to the parents.

The statement should cover the responsibilities of the parents and the agency, and the conditions on which service will be given, including, at a minimum,

- the purpose of the service
- responsibility for financial support
- medical arrangements
- visiting plans
- expectations of the service for the child, including anticipated duration of service
- plans for service for the parents through regular interviews with the social worker or other social and community services
- the understanding that the discharge of the child will be made by prior agreement of the agency, the parents and the child, so that everyone can be suitably prepared

In placements made on court order, a written memorandum of the rights and responsibilities of the parents as defined by the court should be in the case record. The parents should receive a copy.

Termination of Group Home Service

Service should be terminated when the parents are again able to carry their responsibilities for the child, when the child requires another service, or when an adolescent becomes emancipated.

2.21 Preparation for termination

Planning for termination of service should begin at the time of application, to help the family and the child work toward achieving the purpose of the service.

Service may be terminated when

- its purpose has been satisfactorily completed

- the reasons the child needed it have changed
- the parent decides to withdraw the child
- another service may be more effective for the child

Agencies cooperating in the placement plan should be involved in planning termination.

2.22 Aftercare services

The social worker should continue to provide service after the child leaves the group home for a period mutually agreed upon with the family or legal guardian, or stipulated by the court.

3

PROGRAM FOR CARE AND TREATMENT

Care, protection and treatment of children in group homes are based on the following:

a therapeutic milieu in the group home, in the context of close interconnection with the community, providing adult models and a quasi-familial climate with interaction among a group of peers, bringing about constructive personal changes;

a range of social services that further growth, maturity and self-reliance by enhancing self-awareness and understanding of community realities, including clarification of the child's relationship with family members through regular visits, family interviews, family therapy or other treatment;

medical care, mental health services, education and, if appropriate, job training necessary to the development and growth of the child;

use of community services and resources by the child to strengthen social skills and self-reliance.

The Milieu of the Group Home

3.1 Influence of the milieu

The milieu of the group home should exert a vital, helpful influence on the children who live there.

As there are relatively small numbers of adults and children in a group home, patterns of daily living should be similar to those commonly found among families. Respect for a child's appearance and personal possessions significantly affects his or her sense of worth and dignity. Adequacy of the quality and quantity of food, shelter and clothing should be assured. Such an environment contributes to an atmosphere of caring and a positive sense of place both within the group home and in the eyes of the community.

A child's preferences for food and clothing should be considered in the day-to-day planning of the group home activities. Care should be taken to see that the child does not encounter such sharp differences in style of life between the child's own home and the group home that confusion ensues.

3.2 Responsibilities of a child in the group home

Each child should be helped to take on appropriate responsibility, to foster self-reliance and self-confidence.

Helping children to grow includes sharing of responsibilities and completion of tasks. This can be accomplished by gradually giving children routine chores or tasks (e.g., keeping their rooms clean, cleaning up in the kitchen after snacks, helping with laundry), as determined by the child's level of competence.

Money for clothing should be held by group home staff, with the child participating in the selection of clothing and personal necessities as appropriate to age and development, until with gradually increasing ability and responsibility, the child can manage his or her own budget. Each child should have a regular personal spending allowance and learn to manage it. The amount and frequency of the allowance should be related to age and specific activities, church and school contributions and other expenses, as well as patterns within the community.

3.3 Need for structure and behavioral expectations

When the child enters the group home, expectations of individual behavior should be discussed.

An important goal of group home care is to help the child learn appropriate self-control. Expectations and discipline indicate concern for the child's welfare and growth, but should not be used to dominate the child. Corporal punishment, solitary confinement and deprivation of food are not acceptable means of discipline.

Clearly understood behavioral expectations that are firm but adaptable to each child's capacities are an essential part of the foundation on which a sound group home service is built. As the child develops, flexible expectations allow for gradual reduction of staff control with a corresponding increase of the child's control.

3.4 The child's participation in the development of house rules

Children in the group home should participate with staff in the development of house rules.

Sharing in the governing of themselves to resolve daily problems enables children to work together. Justification for rules should be interpreted and emphasized; namely, that people living together need codes to govern their behavior toward each other. There should be as few rules as possible, and the necessity for each rule should be understood and clearly established. A written manual of basic rules may be useful to the children.

3.5 Differential application of rules

Rules should be explicit, consistent and sufficiently flexible for individual treatment of each child.

Although group home living requires more structure, rules and controls than a family home, the children should know that each child is considered an individual with some needs that must be met in individual ways.

Some children with little self-control require clear outside control to live reasonably orderly lives. Increasing maturity of such children should reduce the reliance on external controls. Recognition of growth can be formalized; e.g., by recognition significant tool in treatment to achieve objectives that may be unattainable in individual relationships.

3.9 Use of group meetings

Regular group meetings should be planned.

Such meetings can help
- to deal with common problems of the group, or the group's problem with a child, or community problems
- to consider formulation of rules, plans and procedures in the group home
- to work through the integration or departure of a child or staff member in the group home
- to develop positive approaches to community participation

3.10 Participants in group meetings

Social workers and administrators may participate in group meetings held by the staff and children, whenever indicated.

It should be clear that the social worker and administrator are involved in many aspects of the life of the child and from time to time may need to participate, particularly when the group deals with its difficulties with one child.

3.11 Balanced participation in recreational activity

A proper balance between internal and external activity should be maintained. This should include both quiet and active recreation.

Although the group home is a community within a community, relationships among the children and with the staff should not attain so much importance that other relationships are excluded. The group home then becomes isolated. A thoughtful balance is needed between the essential and valuable internal relationships among the group and the desirable important relationships of the children with those outside the group home— friends, relatives, teachers, recreation leaders, other groups, etc.

of the child's ability to study, return to the home at reasonable hours, etc.

3.6 Attitude and behavior of group home staff

The conduct of group home staff should be a positive model of adult behavior toward the children and the community, and among themselves.

The adult model is one of the helpful influences—perhaps the most indelible—that the milieu exerts on the child.

Staff act in many different roles: surrogate parent, teacher, home manager, etc. Some children have encountered few adults with whom they could identify or after whom they would wish to pattern their own lives. Some children may be wary and suspicious of adults, and even hostile toward them. Staff have to help these children with patience, firmness, dependability and humor. The group home staff can provide a positive pattern that children accept in their maturation.

3.7 Aspects of group interaction

Group home interaction should be planned as an integral part of the intervention needed by the child.

The influence of a group of peers, particularly adolescents, on each other in a group setting cannot be overestimated. Impacts on an individual result simply from the fact of living together, with the constant pressure for involvement and socialization: sharing a room, eating as a group, even such elementary necessities as limiting the length of conversations, or relinquishing the bathroom. Peers can often be more blunt in approval or criticism of a child than group home staff.

3.8 Group interaction as a therapeutic medium

Continuous efforts should be made to assist the children in the group home to form a viable and dynamic group.

The dynamics of group authority and influence can be a

3.12 Number of children in the group home

The number of children in each group home should be determined by such considerations as physical facilities, neighborhood conditions, staffing and administrative structure, as well as the developmental levels and the program and treatment needs of the children in the group.

A group home should not be used for fewer than five children or more than 12. A group of six to eight children is optimum because it is small enough to allow for individualization and large enough to remain a group even if a member is absent (e.g., visiting at home).

3.13 Composition of the group

The children in the group home should complement each other to form a viable group.

In the grouping of unrelated children, care should be taken to achieve beneficial consequences, or to avoid negative results, for each member of the group. However, group homes developed for highly specialized reasons, e.g., diagnostic purposes or other short-term programs, such as care of runaways, may not have to focus as carefully on group composition. The purpose of the group home service, therefore, should determine the mix of children. When long-term placement is planned, children with some common characteristics (e.g., age, verbal ability, developmental stage) are more likely to be compatible.

3.14 Coed group home

Group homes that provide care and service to boys and girls should plan for the development of positive social relationships between the sexes.

Experience with coed groups has demonstrated that boys and girls under the age of 12 usually live together with minimum difficulties.

Some group homes for adolescent boys and girls have been established. Reports of those experiences are mixed. Careful planning in relation to the physical facilities, number of children and quality of supervision has led to positive social relationships in many homes. Some adolescents are seen to be in need of a home that minimizes the sexual tensions and anxieties that occur at this stage of development. The kinds of problem and the level of disturbance of the adolescents are determining factors.

Integration of Social Services

3.15 Intake

The child and the parents should be seen by the social worker, group home staff, group home supervisor and appropriate specialists.

Mutual evaluation should consider the developmental level of the child, the child-parent relationship, readiness to separate from each other, and consideration of entrance into a group home.

3.16 Joint decision on provision of service

The decision of the agency to place the child in a group home and the plan of service should be based on pooled information. (2.3)

Social service staff should confer with staff of the group home as well as consider the information obtained during the intake study. The presence of any special problems and the composition of the group in residence have to be considered in deciding whether a particular child can benefit from placement in a particular group home. The child should participate in the process as soon as there are indications that a group home service may be suitable, and should meet the staff in the group home.

3.17 Introduction to placement

Social services, group home staff and supervisor or the family group home parents should jointly plan the beginning period of placement, with the age, maturity and previous experiences of the child in mind.

>Arrangements should be made for increasingly lengthened preadmission visits by the child before the actual move into the group home.

>The parents should accompany the child to the group home. The social worker and group home supervisor must offer sensitive help to the child and parents in relation to their feelings about the proposed change.

3.18 Planning and evaluating use of the service

A systematic process of planning, evaluation and reassessment of the value of the service should be established with the child and the parents. (2.9, 2.13)

>Focus should be on the questions whether service maintains and strengthens the child appropriately, whether the child or family needs help of a different kind, and whether another plan may be more suitable.

>Social service staff and group home staff should have regular conferences, formal and informal, to exchange observations and information about the children and families in order to determine the general direction of work in individual situations. It is important for the social services worker to see the group home records of the behavior of the children to maintain constant awareness of their development.

3.19 Preparation for termination

Planning for termination of the service should begin at the time of application to help the child and family use the service purposefully, and should include help to the family in reassuming its responsibilities or in making another plan. (2.9)

>All staff, insofar as possible, should help prepare the child as carefully for leaving as they did for entering the group home, with sufficient time allowed.

Professional Services

3.20 Responsibility for medical care

Responsibility for regular medical care should be delegated to the agency responsible for the child's physical care. (6.31)

3.21 Availability of medical care

The agency should have available a physician, preferably from the community, for the regular care of the children.

> Staff members responsible for the care of children with special health needs should receive training that ensures proper handling and use of medicines and prescriptions, as well as other forms of health care.
>
> Medication should be given only on written order of the physician.
>
> Exceptions may occur with the occasional use of such remedies as analgesics, local skin lotions, or Band Aids, for a day or two.
>
> All medication and toxic substances given to a child should be recorded in that child's health record. (4.20)
>
> Medication programs should be reviewed regularly by the physician. The physician should provide consultation to the staff to help them understand health problems of children and to deal with allergic reactions and emergency situations. Staff should know first aid.

3.22 Provision for medical care

Provision should be made for prompt medical care in cases of suspected illness and emergencies and for diagnosis and treatment of any physical illness or handicap.

> The child's regular physician should provide emergency as well as regular care.

3.23 Care of a sick child in the group home

A child who becomes ill should be cared for in the group home as long as this is medically and socially desirable.

Because children—especially placed children—are often fearful and unhappy in strange surroundings, removal from the group home should occur only when necessary for medical reasons or when the care required is so taxing that staff are not able to care for the other children adequately.

When a child shows the first signs of a contagious illness, the other children have already been exposed. Staff should be alert to all signs of illness.

3.24 Hospitalization

Provision should be made and procedures established for hospitalization of children when required (including emergencies) through arrangement by the regular physician with local hospitals where adequate medical care is available.

3.25 Health records

An individual health record should be maintained for each child who enters care.

The record should contain a report of the preadmission physical examinations and recommendations, previous medical and health history, including serious past illnesses, infectious diseases, current medical problems, medications, chronic illness, allergies and other important medical information, and observations on the child's nutrition. The health record should include

- reports of tests, immunizations (including the date of last tetanus injection), yearly reexaminations and recommendations
- group home staff notes regarding health care
- reports of mental health and neurological examinations and psychological reports when applicable

- results of dental, eye, hearing and other examinations and consultations, dates of treatment and by whom given

A signed parental authorization for regular and emergency medical and surgical care, for immunizations, and hospitalization when indicated, should be on file in the medical record. For elective hospitalization and surgery, a consent for the specific procedure should be obtained from the parent. (2.20)

3.26 Mental health services

Mental health services should be available for diagnosis, consultation and treatment of children when indicated.

Mental health services should be provided to children

- who give evidence of serious personal disturbance previous to or during intake and while under care
- who, because of personality difficulties, may be unable to use group home service before admission or while in the group home, in order to plan a more appropriate form of care or treatment
- when requested by social service or the group home supervisor for periodic evaluation of progress or treatment of an individual child
- when an individual staff member requires consultation because of his or her responsibility for direct treatment of a child, and for formulating or modifying the service treatment or plan

Inservice training of staff, should be carried on to help staff strengthen their understanding of developmental and symptomatic behavior in order to deal with it in a way that is best for the child.

Use should be made of mental health services and facilities in the community when they are available.

3.27 Psychological services

A psychologist should be available to contribute to diagnosis and formulation of a plan of care and treatment for children who enter the group home or are living there.

The psychologist should
- assist in the formulation of a plan for help to a child with learning difficulties, where evaluation of educational achievement and potential of a child is needed
- administer psychological tests as needed
- work with individual children when indicated
- consult with the staff

Community Services

3.28 Education

Each child should be helped to obtain as much formal education as he or she is able to use.

Optimum conditions should be provided for the child to obtain the greatest benefit from his schooling experience.

The agency is responsible for children's attendance at school full-time throughout the period required by law, and in general until they are 16 years old.

Completion of high school is preferred. Children or youth whose aptitudes, personality and school record show ability to profit from further education should be enabled to do so.

Children residing in group homes should be able to attend regular community schools. There are, however, exceptions to the foregoing. A child with learning problems or coming from a residential placement may need to attend specialized educational facilities within the school system, or to receive special tutoring either in the school or group home.

A child with a good school adjustment who enters a group home that is not too far from the school that he attended may wish and should be able to remain in his regular school. Many children who have lived away from home have had several changes of schools; another change should be avoided whenever possible, particularly if the placement occurs during the school year or is for a brief period. It may also be desirable for the children in the group home to attend different schools to further their identity as distinct individuals.

3.29   Staff relationship to school personnel

Group home staff should cooperate with school personnel to further the child's progress in school.

School personnel may need help to understand the purpose and goals of group home service and its care of children. Every opportunity should be used to enlist their interest. Child care staff should participate as much as possible in community school activities, and attend PTA meetings and school programs, especially when a child participates.

The social worker or selected group home staff (or both when necessary) should be available for conferences with school personnel throughout the school year.

3.30   Helping children with schoolwork

A child who needs individual help and instruction should have the assistance of group home staff and, where necessary, of a tutor.

A child who has made several changes of school may need special help to adapt to a new school. When remedial instruction is necessary, it should be provided by the group home if it is not available in the school.

Staff can offer help with homework and discussions about current and former schools. Tutoring should supplement school attendance, not substitute for it.

The agency should make resources available for children who need special help because of particular learning difficulties.

3.31   Development of special interests

Opportunities for the development of cultural or other special interests or talents should be available to the children who live in the group home.

Provision should be made for private instruction, special classes, participation in community activities for children interested in music, fine arts, dancing, crafts, swimming and other sports, etc.

3.32 Vocational counseling and training

Children of high school age should be prepared for economic independence.

Available community facilities should be used for vocational counseling and training.

Both the social worker and vocational counselor should help the child in selection of appropriate occupation and/or training course. If attendance at college is appropriate, the agency should take the responsibility for helping the child obtain funds for this.

3.33 Recreational activities

Group home staff should encourage and assist the child to engage in community recreation according to the child's interests and abilities.

The activity needs of children should be considered and planned in the daily routine of the group home. Activities serve as a channel for energy, and for stimulation of relationships with others. Recreational activity also assists children to make choices, solve problems and develop physically. Time should also be available for children to be alone, to engage in solitary activities such as reading, cycling, and other hobbies. There should also be time and opportunity for spontaneous group activities such as singing, dancing, listening to records.

Use of television may have to be guided by rules about the hours when viewing is allowed and types of program to be viewed.

3.34 Recreational equipment

Games, toys and athletic equipment should be selected and provided according to the ages, needs and interests of the children.

Materials for creative activities and specially purchased equipment should be obtained with the needs of the children in mind.

Equipment owned in common, such as games, should be easily accessible in the group home, and the children's personal possessions should be safely their own.

4

THE PHYSICAL STRUCTURE OF THE GROUP HOME

The total environment of the group home should convey to each child a sense of personal worth, and entitlement to a safe and pleasant home.

It should be indistinguishable from typical homes in a neighborhood that contains a variety of potentially beneficial influences. It should be designed to meet the needs and characteristics of the children who will live there.

Relationships With the Community When Establishing a Group Home

Planning for effective relationships with the community in the development of group home service is a necessary responsibility of the agency.

4.1 Community assessment

The agency should assess the community and specific neighborhoods before selecting a residence and an environment appropriate for the children who will live there.

> Community opposition to the establishment of a group home is not uncommon. The agency must evaluate the degree, meaning and consequences of any opposition in order to determine its potential effect on the welfare of the children.
>
> Information should be gathered about the social and economic

makeup of the area to determine whether the children to be served by the group home will be able to be accepted, make friends and become a part of the community. Many communities or neighborhoods have views about the kinds of child who have created problems in the past. The history of any struggles of other agencies or organizations should be weighed. Community services, formal and informal leadership, and possible community support should be approached.

4.2 Initial approach to the community

When a specific home has been found, the agency should decide upon its initial approach to the community on the basis of its assessment.

The approach should be guided in each instance by what will diminish the community's feeling of distance and estrangement and, optimally, what will increase feelings of social responsibility for children. As opportunities will be needed for social, recreational, educational, work and other activities, this may require early and active involvement with the community. Its tolerance or diminishing resistance may not be sufficient.

In a heterogeneous or highly urbanized and transitional community, the residence may not be anticipated fearfully before its establishment, and will be judged on its integration into the community and how well it is run. The residence may be located in some of such communities the way a family home is located, without further identification.

In a well established, socially cohesive residential community, where municipal officials and other community leaders exercise a great deal of influence, and constituents usually endorse their views, contact with significant public officials and professionals is recommended.

A combined approach to community leaders and immediate neighbors is preferable in communities where individuals and groups expect to participate in decisions about use of property and about the residents who live there. The agency should contact community persons who have demonstrated interest in the well-being of children and are likely to support the service: the social welfare planning council, the mental health catchment area council, citizens' groups and individuals concerned about and interested in the development of children's services. The program should be explained clearly as to its objectives, screening and selection criteria, degree and type of supervision, and procedures used in critical situations.

4.3 Response to community concerns

A supervisor, administrator or manager of the group home service should respond quickly to criticism about the children in the group home or the group home staff.

Even with a thorough assessment, thoughtful decisions and use of the best approach to entering the community, intervening factors and forces may cause community resistance to a group home. Direct mediation should be an ongoing practice in each agency that provides group home service.

Sensitive, realistic clarification of the issues, and negotiations between the parties give both sides an opportunity to express their concerns and exchange ideas. This can facilitate better understanding and mutual adjustment.

4.4 Coordination with regulatory and standard-setting agencies

An administrative staff person should be responsible for coordinating all contacts with regulatory and standard-setting agencies to save time and facilitate inspections of the group home.

Choosing the Group Home

4.5 Group home as a family residence

The living unit should be a homelike residence in good repair in a residential area.

Many residential areas are zoned for families. Zoning regulations for families should include group homes operated by an agency as family dwellings. Individual variances or exceptions should be sought when necessary.

The handling of zoning problems calls for interpretation of the needs of the children and the value of group home service for them. The community should be made aware that the agency selects responsible staff to care for a small group of children who both need and value life in the community, and further, that the agency has carefully determined that each of the children can benefit from this service.

Problems about the noise and activity of the children may be avoided by a preference for rental units on the first floor, or for detached homes. Sound-absorbing materials for ceilings and carpeting, etc., are also beneficial, particularly if the home is adjacent to others or in an apartment building.

4.6 Stability of the living unit

Stability of the group home should be assured by the agency whether it purchases or rents the facility.

Children who have had little stability in their lives need assurance that they have a home as long as they require it.

Ownership permits the agency to assure stability to the children who must use group home service. It allows freedom to make structural changes to suit the needs of the children the agency will serve. When the agency rents or leases, efforts should also be made to assure children the same security. Renting property provides the opportunity to move from an unsuitable home or area without serious financial loss.

4.7 Neighborhood facilities in selection of the group home

The location of the group home should be convenient to needed facilities.

The group home should be within a reasonable distance of or have access to
- schools for children at different levels of educational

achievement, including specialized educational facilities, and technical and vocational schools

- public transportation or other convenient transportation to agency offices
- places of worship that correspond to the various faiths of the children
- recreation, cultural facilities and social groups that accord with the interest of the children
- part-time job opportunities (gas stations, food markets, baby-sitting)
- shopping facilities for daily operation of the living unit
- health services for medical care and treatment, as well as medical emergencies

School-age children are likely to explore their own neighborhoods and participate in school activities. If there is question about the safety of the neighborhood, special arrangements to ensure the safety of the children should be made. Movement of adolescents into the larger community will require access to transportation systems.

The Group Home

The group home should have adequate space for all phases of daily living, including recreation, privacy, group activities and visits from community acquaintances and friends.

Choice and arrangement of furnishings and equipment for the children contribute to the quality of the service by making children more comfortable and secure, inviting their interest, promoting cooperative endeavors and suggesting both quiet and active functioning.

4.8 Arrangement of living units

Renovation or construction of the group home should be designed to provide for each group of children the rooms and space needed.

It should be easy and natural for the group to join the staff at various times during the day. The opportunity to do so enhances a child's feeling of having a place and a group to which the child belongs. Rooms used by the children should be conveniently grouped. Staff rooms should permit unobtrusive observation of the children day and night.

4.9 Living room

A living room should be available for children to gather for reading, study, relaxation and entertaining.

The living room should be a cozy, attractive and inviting place in which a child can take pride. Books, magazines and newspapers, television, stereo sets, plants and flowers help to create a homelike atmosphere.

4.10 Recreation, space and leisure

Recreation areas should be adapted to the specific needs of the children and to neighborhood patterns.

A group home should assure adequate space for games, individual hobbies and active play. In densely populated communities space may include use of community facilities nearby. Less densely populated areas may have to incorporate more space within and depend less on outside facilities.

Materials for arts, hobbies and crafts should be in accordance with the cultural, educational and personal interests of the children and be easily accessible to them. Storage space is advisable for these materials, and for sports equipment.

4.11 Dining area

The dining area should be arranged and equipped so that the children can have their meals together and mealtime can be an enjoyable experience.

Attractive dishes, silverware, placemats or tablecloths, and napkins add dignity to mealtimes and encourage children to develop orderly living habits and manners.

4.12 Bedrooms

Sufficient single and double bedrooms should be available for flexible use.

Each child should be able to have and enjoy some privacy alone or with friends, as well as with some groupings.

Single bedrooms should be available for those children prone to overstimulation, and particularly for adolescents, who often prefer to have a room of their own. To enhance individuality and a sense of worth and responsibility, a child should have a chest of drawers, table or desk, a closet with clothes racks and shelves within easy reach, and a place for individual personal possessions. A good mirror in each room is also helpful.

All sleeping rooms should be outside rooms, well ventilated, adequately lighted, heated and cooled according to climate. Each child should have a separate bed, a clean and comfortable mattress, bedding appropriate to the weather and climate, and a plastic mattress cover or other protection when necessary.

4.13 Bath and toilet facilities

There should be a sufficient number of separate toilet and bathing facilities for children and staff.

To be adequate, facilities should promote privacy and convenience, i. e., easy access to sleeping, living and recreation rooms. The mix of bathrooms, showers and toilet facilities will vary according to the age and needs of the children who will live in the home. An important aspect of planning the group home is the extent to which it facilitates health and personal hygiene and assists the children to live together as individuals.

The children should have a designated place for their own

items of personal care such as toothbrush, towel and washcloth.

4.14 Kitchen

The group home should have a sufficiently well equipped kitchen to prepare meals for children and staff.

Size, amount and kind of equipment should be determined by the needs and the number of persons in the group home.

A well equipped kitchen is essential to good service and helpful to children who are learning about food preparation. There should be appropriate storage for supplies. The kitchen should be well lighted and equipped for control of heat and odors. Cleaning supplies and equipment should be stored apart from food. Full compliance with local and state fire and safety regulations regarding the kind and arrangement of kitchen equipment is essential.

4.15 Equipment

General utility equipment, including labor-saving devices, that provides easy maintenance of the home should be kept in good repair and should be readily accessible.

A washing machine, dryer, iron, ironing board and other equipment for suitable care of clothing help children to become adept enough to participate in daily household tasks with adequate supervision. Use of commercial laundry services should be evaluated in terms of the needs of the children and the most feasible plan for maintenance of the home.

The group home should have a comfortable, ventilated and well lit utility area for storage of equipment.

Adequate storage space for household supplies, games and sports equipment, crafts supplies, frequently used household furnishings, and clothing, bedding and linen should be conveniently within reach of the group home staff.

4.16 Furnishings

Furnishings should be appropriate to the age and activities of the children in the group, as well as attractive and easy to clean.

Household furnishings, curtains, rugs and pictures should be chosen with the children's interest and safety in mind. Colors for the walls or floor coverings should take into consideration the importance of the impact of color on children and adults. Whenever possible, the children should be encouraged to contribute their ideas to the decoration of the group home.

Well made furnishings should be sturdy and durable enough for the use and comfort of the children, and should take into account any special characteristics of the children, such as disabilities, as well as activities related to the community, such as visits and parties.

4.17 Living accommodations for group home staff

A staff member who is on duty and sleeping in should have at least a room with a bed and bath reserved for personal use.

Staff rooms should be close to the children's rooms so that supervision is easy and staff is available to any child when needed day or night.

It is preferable for staff to maintain their own residence away from the group home when they work in an agency-controlled group home.

Agency service, however, may include a married couple as the group home staff who assume responsibility for the group home and live there. Their privacy should be ensured by their having their own living room, bedroom and bath when they are not on duty.

4.18 Family-owned group home

Family-owned group homes should meet the same expectations for physical arrangements as those owned or rented by the agency.

The group home should be designed or arranged for a group of children to have sufficient space and provide appropriate privacy for the adults and children who live there.

4.19 Maintenance

There should be a plan and budgetary provision for regular maintenance and replacement of all equipment and furnishings to ensure adequate living conditions.

The group home, its premises and equipment should be kept clean, sanitary and in good repair at all times.

Daily maintenance of the group home should be encouraged by use of materials that are attractive and easy to clean. Hot and cold running water should always be available. Floors should be warm and easily cleaned.

The telephone number of regularly used repair services should be posted conspicuously.

4.20 Safety and sanitation

The group home should be structurally sound, safe for children, and as fire resistant as possible.

As a minimum, buildings, heating, water supply, sewage disposal, lighting, ventilation, food preparation, fire protection, and other health and safety measures must comply with the codes and ordinances established by the state, the county and city where the group home is located. Regulations differ with locations. Where regular inspection of the premises by licensing authorities is not required by law, it should be requested yearly by the agency to assure safety.

Group homes that care for children with limited physical or mental abilities need more safety systems and devices for their protection. Consultation with appropriate public officials should be sought in such circumstances.

All toxic substances and medications should be out of reach of the children. Medications should be under lock and key, available only under staff supervision. (3.21)

A group home should have a non-coin telephone; no time should be lost in an emergency.

5

STAFFING THE GROUP HOME

In the continuum of child placement resources, a group home occupies a place as one of the residential services. In these standards, the term group home staff will be used to designate the adults in charge of the daily living of the children and the direct operation of the group home.

5.1 Employment of adults in charge of the group home

The social agency should base its decision about the kind of group home staff required according to the purpose of the service and the needs of the children who are or will be placed in the group home.

The abilities of staff, the number of children, the variety of ages, sex and other characteristics should all be considered in making this decision.

5.2 One or more staff members should be in the group home at all times.

Staffing and patterns of responsibility are different from those in larger facilities providing care and service for children.

The number of staff members caring for the children will vary in response to the group of children and their individual needs, circumstances associated with operation of the home, and the nature of the services, treatment and collaboration with other professionals. (6.39)

The availability of two or more staff members will be necessary for children who are physically or mentally handicapped or in need of protection to ensure attention to their needs and adequate response to emergencies and unexpected situations. The greater the number of children in the group home, the larger the number of staff that will be required. Even in the smallest group home, more than one staff member must be present when most of the children are at home.

5.3 Time off for group home staff

Provision should be made for group home staff to have the equivalent of 2 days off weekly.

> Operating a group home is demanding. Adequate time off is essential for the staff to maintain freshness and creativity.
>
> A variety of work schedules can be devised for unrelated group home staff; however, no group home worker should be in sole charge of the house and children for more than 40 consecutive hours.
>
> When a married couple operate a group home and one mate is routinely away from the home during the day, and the children are also normally away from home during the day, the other partner may manage the house during the day with the help of auxiliary staff to assist after school or if a child is ill.
>
> A child should not be responsible for the care of other children.

5.4 Coordination of the operation of the group home

Schedules of group home staff should provide time on a regular basis for discussion and coordination of plans for the care of the children, management of the home and communication with other staff both in the group home and, as indicated, in the agency office.

> Time should also be planned for regular supervision and inservice training.

5.5 Other group home personnel

Responsibilities should be defined for supplementary staff—for example, tutors, recreation workers, college students and volunteers with special skills, including areas such as music, handicrafts, etc. Their responsibilities should be defined by the agency in conjunction with those of persons who manage the group home.

In addition to the basic responsibility of assisting group home staff, specific duties may be assigned, such as

• escorting children to special events

• individual help for a child who is seeking employment, applying to college or following a medical or therapeutic regimen

Supplementary staff should be familiar with the children as well as the group home and its routine and atmosphere.

Use of specialized personnel (e. g., recreation workers) whose functions duplicate those available in the community runs counter to the intent that the children use community resources to stimulate outside relationships and familiarity with community patterns.

Responsibility of Group Home Staff

5.6 Agency expectations of group home staff

Staff responsible for the care and protection of the children in the group home should maintain a home that is comfortable, secure, safe and reasonably harmonious for the children who live there.

The group home staff achieves an adequately functioning home through the ability to meet daily living requirements of household management; housekeeping; money management; scheduling of meals; working and sleeping patterns; and the many problems that arise daily in caring for a group of children.

This task calls for

• meeting role requirements as heads of a household

• supplying love, care, guidance, supervision, discipline, authority, protection and role models that children need

• providing experiences of continuous and dependable emotional relationships paced and responsive to the changing needs of the child

• providing learning and socialization experiences (including values and standards of social behavior), experiences of how adult and family roles and functions are carried out; stimulation of senses, mind and potentials

- protecting the child and helping him learn to protect himself from degrading and dangerous experiences
- offering sources of cultural enrichment as part of daily living

Techniques used to influence children's behavior must protect children's basic rights and needs for food, clothing, allowances, etc.

The group home staff carried primary responsiblity for protecting and promoting the physical and mental health of each child while in the home.

The group home staff should offer help to each child in educational and vocational opportunities for

- learning knowledge and skill, modes of behavior, values
- developing special interests and talents
- learning how to earn a living

Recruitment of Group Home Staff

It is necessary for the agency to formulate a plan for the recruitment and employment of its group home staff. The success of the group home program depends in largest measure on the kind of staff employed, their competence and stability.

5.7 Sources of recruitment

Several sources for recruitment of staff should be explored.

Sources include acquaintances of personnel employed by the agency; associations of child care personnel; colleges and specialized schools for the training of child care workers; and graduate schools of universities, when the agency employs graduate students as married couples.

Advertisements in newspapers and child welfare publications may be used.

Individuals who live in the neighborhood of the group home

not only may be qualified but may have the advantage of community ties that can assist a child in strange surroundings.

Supervision

The agency should ensure maintenance of professional standards of service and professional quality of care in the group home.

5.8 Supervision in the group home

Supervision should offer guidance and support to the staff in caring for the children. (6.25)

Group home staff should have access to supervisory assistance at all times, in addition to regular supervisory conferences.

Considerable variability and diversity occur in carrying out responsibility for supervision of a group home. Flexibility in terms of time schedules, tasks and functions, with few rules and a minimum of standardized procedures, is advisable.

The skills and knowledge of the supervisor in the group home should be used to

- consider means of improving care and service for the children
- discuss agency policies and practices with staff
- enhance and strengthen the ability of staff to meet daily problems of management with competence and confidence
- prevent and/or deter problems in care of the children or management of the group home
- whenever indicated, communicate and establish relationships with other community institutions (e. g., schools, medical resources, community leaders) in behalf of the children
- encourage positive and productive relationships with staff in the group home and with other agency staff
- allow for mobilization of resources, i. e., emergency medical care

6

ORGANIZATION AND ADMINISTRATION OF AGENCIES PROVIDING GROUP HOME SERVICE

Regardless of auspices, the agency that makes group home service available to a child must be organized to ensure that each child gets the care and protection he needs and the social work services to foster the development of the child and assist the parents. The achievement of this goal depends upon
- caliber and conviction of the governing body
- adequacy of financing
- qualifications of the staff
- continuing staff development within the agency
- coordination of all the components of the service and integration of the activities of the various staff members
- collaborative relationships in the community

Each agency must define the purposes and goals of its services, the type of group home service it intends to provide, the ages and numbers of the children it will care for and the policies and procedures governing its services. These will be determined by the auspices and the resources, both professional and financial, of the agency, and should be developed on the basis of community needs.

6.1 Auspices

Group home service, as a child welfare service, should be administered by an authorized public or voluntary social agency, which may offer group home service as its only function or as one of its multiple services for children and families.

It should be recognized that many special services can be provided under the same auspices, within a multiservice agency. It is also possible for one agency to provide different kinds of service in different group homes according to the special needs of the children.

6.2 Authorization

The voluntary agency should be authorized by the state department responsible for child welfare services to provide group home service, and should function with a duly constituted charter and by-laws, in accordance with the legal requirements of the state, county or city.

6.3 Incorporation

The voluntary agency should be incorporated under state and local requirements. The public agency should be properly authorized by law to administer group home service.

6.4 The group home as a social agency

The group home that assumes total responsibility for providing a group home service should be incorporated and administered as a social agency and should offer services in accordance with standards for all other social agencies providing such services.

6.5 Licensing of group homes

All group homes should be licensed and authorized to operate by the appropriate state agency.

Board of Directors

The voluntary agency should have a board of directors that operates as the governing body of the agency. Although the public agency may differ from the voluntary agency in structure and responsibility based on statutory requirements, it is important for the public agency to have active citizen participation in providing group home service through a policy-making board or an advisory committee.

6.6 Composition of the board (of a voluntary agency) or advisory committee (of a public agency)

A governing board or advisory committee should be drawn from a broad spectrum of the community.

Membership should include diversity of age, race, sex and representation from professional, labor, business and other groups such as potential or former consumers.

To avoid conflict of interest, there should be no business transactions between members and the agency.

6.7 Qualifications of board or advisory committee members

Board or committee members should be selected who are concerned about the service and the children served by the agency and who are informed or wish to become informed about group home service and the principles on which it is based.

Board members should have

- imagination and intelligence
- an interest in and commitment to the objectives of the agency
- willingness and ability to participate responsively in the duties of the board or the advisory committee
- capacity to interest other people and work with them as an advocate for good services for children and their families
- concern about social conditions in the community that affect the welfare of children

6.8 Change of board composition

There should be a plan for periodic change of composition of the board or advisory committee that will assure an active, enlightened and effective body with various points of view as well as continuity of purpose and long-range goals.

This may be achieved by

- provision for rotation of all members on an overlapping basis or by assigning responsibility to a nominating committee to propose and retain only those board members who have been effective

6.9 Responsibility of a governing board

The board should be responsible for developing the program, formulating policies and assuring adequate financial support of services offered by the agency.

These responsibilities include

- accounting to the community for its stewardship in regard to the service of the agency and the administration of agency funds
- interpreting the program, policies and financial needs of the agency to the community at large, to fund-raising groups, and to groups responsible for making budgetary appropriations
- evaluating the agency's function and services periodically in relation to changing needs in the community, modifying or expanding services where necessary
- selecting and employing a properly qualified executive director to whom responsibility for administration of the service is delegated
- assuring desirable personnel practices for recruitment and retention of staff and reasonable salaries or compensation
- being informed about unmet needs in the community and bringing them to the agency's attention

6.10 Responsibility of an advisory committee

An advisory committee of a public agency should fulfill several important functions.

The committee is responsible for
- recommending policies and changes of policies and needed services
- interpreting the service to the community
- obtaining community support for the program
- assuring adequate standards for the service through citizen action

Agency Policies and Procedures

6.11 Formulation of policies

Policies and procedures should be formulated in writing by the board and staff.

The agency's purpose and the community's need for the group home service should furnish the basis for the policies and procedures.

6.12 Evaluation of services

The agency should study its provision of group home service.

The study should
- ensure that care and service provided are in accordance with the purposes of service for each child
- assess the adequacy and efficiency of agency resources to carry out the objectives of group home service
- assure that the service carries out the intent of the agency in making it available

6.13 Procedures for appeals

The agency should provide workable procedures that can be readily used on behalf of the child when care or services or plans are deemed unsatisfactory.

These procedures should be made known to parents, agency staff and older children.

If a voluntary agency is providing the service through a contract with a public agency, provision should be made for complaints to be lodged first with the administrative staff of the agency providing the service and then, if necessary, with the public agency ultimately responsible for the child.

6.14   Assumption of legal responsibility

The agency that makes group home service available for a child in its own program or through purchase of service should be empowered to do so by voluntary agreement with the parent or legal custodian or guardian, or through judicial action.

The public agency as well as the voluntary agency should be able to accept children directly from their parents or guardians whenever parents are capable of making appropriate plans for the child.

Routine or arbritary abridgment of parental rights by judicial action should not be a requirement for receiving service from the agency. If abridgment is necessary for the welfare of the child, the agency should assume only those rights that are essential for its service and should operate consistently within the framework of the rights it has assumed and the rights that the child's parents retain.

6.15   Legal status of child

In accepting a child for group home care, the agency should be responsible for determining who has legal custody or guardianship, especially in instances where parents are separated, divorced or unmarried, or when the child is committed by court.

Planning for each child should explicitly take into account his legal relationship to the parents or guardian and the agency or agencies providing service.

The agency should make certain that for each child there is a legally responsible individual who exercises right of guardianship of the person.

If termination of parental rights or determination of guardianship becomes necessary because of death or unavailability of a parent, the agency should be prepared to initiate appropriate court proceedings.

The agency should have in its files valid documentation of a child's legal status from a proper court, or a written agreement from the parent, that establishes the child's custody and authorizes his placement by the agency.

6.16 Budget

The agency should have sufficient financial resources and a budget that enables it to serve the children it cares for in accordance with approved standards of practice.

The annual budget of an agency should be used for its own administrative purpose, to inform community funding bodies and the public about unmet needs in the community, and to account for quality and effectiveness of its service.

6.17 Sources of support

Financial support for group home service should be derived from voluntary contributions, community funds, tax funds, endowments and parents' fees.

It is preferable for the voluntary agency to have multiple sources of financing. Purchase of care for individual children by another agency should meet the full cost of care and service.

6.18 Analysis of costs

Yearly cost analysis should provide an informed picture that can be used as the basis for decisions about services.

The cost analysis should

- yield information needed by the agency to keep in step with changing needs of the children requiring service and of the community it serves
- provide a sound base for entering into agreements for purchase of service and reimbursement of costs

6.19 Determinants of average cost for a child using group home service

The cost of care and service for a child should be determined by the basic cost of maintaining a child; the standard of living in the community in regard to recreational, social, educational and cultural experiences; and administrative expenses.

Three types of expenditure are suggested: direct expenditures for the care and service for a child, prorated expenditure for the maintenance of the group home, and administrative expenditures.

Direct expenditures for care of a child include cost of food, clothing, health care and treatment, education, recreation, transportation and carfare allowances, special expenses to meet unusual needs.

Expenditures for each group home include salaries or contractual fees for all staff in the group home, rent (if the agency does not own the group home), property and water taxes when applicable, mortgage payments, repairs to property, insurances, telephone and other utilities, automobile cost for children and staff, repairs and maintenance of the group home and household equipment, household supplies and laundry.

Administrative costs include salaries for administrative, consultative and office staff; cost of staff development; general office expenses; rent and telephone; bank, trust company, audit and accounting fees; indirect services of the parent organization.

6.20 Determinants of average cost for a child using family group home service

If the care is in a family group home, prorated costs to be calculated are as noted (6.19), as well as special expenses to meet unusual needs of the children.

Costs applicable to family group home operating care are
- prorated costs of housing, heat, utilities, insurance, telephone, household and cleaning supplies, laundry, maintenance and repairs
- repairs and replacement of household equipment and furnishings
- supplies for services to the children
- extra household help

Donated goods and services should be given an estimated value in order to reflect actual cost of services and arrive at a true figure.

The agency should assume responsibility for payments to the family group home to ensure stability and to maintain its own responsibility for the care of the child.

If the parents are able to pay part or all of the cost of care, these payments should be made to the agency paying the cost.

6.21 Determinants of cost for a child with special needs using group services

Basic costs for group home or family group home service should be calculated as noted (6.19 and 6.20).

Special costs for care, service and treatment should be calculated according to actual costs. These might include special diet, special clothing, additional transportation, special tutoring, additional group home staff.

6.22 Administrative structure

The structure of administration, the lines of responsibility, and job descriptions of the group home supervisor and the social worker should be clearly defined, particularly in a multiservice agency.

Responsibility for the group home service should reside in one person, to whom specific duties are assigned. The supervisor of the group home service or, in a small agency, the executive or social work supervisor, should carry this responsibility. Responsibility for children receiving family group home service may be carried by the group home service unit, or may be assigned to social workers in different units in a multiservice agency.

6.23 Size of staff

The agency should provide qualified social work and group home staff in sufficient number to offer the quality of service that will effectively meet the needs of children and families who come to the attention of the agency. (6.35)

Decisions about the number of adults needed should be based on the number of children in the group home, their age, the complexity of their problems, and the amount of services needed.

Variables taken into account to determine the size of staff include

• nature of the problems and other characteristics of children accepted for care

• number of cases in which intensive work with children and/or parents is required

• amount of time required for individual and staff conferences

• amount of time required for consultation

• responsibilities other than direct work with children or parents, such as community activities and administrative responsibilities

6.24 Administrative responsibility for the group home

Administrative responsibility lies with both the agency operating the group home and the agency purchasing group home care to ensure that adequate care and service is given.

Directly or by delegation this responsibility includes
• recruitment, employment, training of group home staff
• assignment of staff to a group home

- supervision of group home staff, including periodic evaluation
- continuous evaluation of applications for service
- suitable selection of a group home for a child
- recommendations for policies including intake and reimbursements
- consultation to agencies that purchase service
- participation in planning and administration of the budget
- maintenance of a system of record keeping for evaluative, statistical and interpretive material
- interpretation of the service and procedures

6.25 Qualifications of the supervisor of the group home staff

The supervisor of the group home staff should have substantial experience in child care and may have professional training in any of the several human service fields. (5.8)

Whether this function is carried by the executive, administrator, or the social work supervisor, supervision of child care staff should be assured.

The workload of the group home supervisor should be adjusted to permit regular weekly conferences, and meetings as needed, to assure sound group home operation and service for the children.

6.26 Qualifications of group home staff

Group home staff should be selected on the basis of their ability to manage the group home, care for the children, and work with other members of the staff. (5.6)

Group home staff should be able to

- meet daily tasks of household management (i.e., housekeeping, money management, routines of meals, sleeping arrangements, school attendance)
- further the development of children in the group home, and

demonstrate knowledge of standards and modes of behavior requisite for living in a cooperative society

• collaborate and share responsibility with other professionals involved with the group home and the children placed there

• involve the children in responsible tasks within the group home and in responsible participation in the neighborhood and the community

• deal with local tradespeople and obtain necessary services and supplies for ongoing maintenance of the group home

• be comfortable with relationships with many different persons, including community volunteers and neighbors, and comfortably convey simple explanations of the group home service

6.27 Physical examination of group home staff

Each member of the group home staff should have a physical examination at agency cost prior to employment. An annual examination should be required thereafter.

With the consent of the staff member, preventive medical tests and measures should be taken as decided upon in consultation with the medical consultant.

6.28 Social workers in group home service

Social workers who carry responsibility for children and families using group home service should have professional social work training, social work experience, and diagnostic and treatment skills in working with children and families.

6.29 Social work supervisor

Responsibility for supervision of social workers for group home service should be carried by the social work supervisor or by the group home staff supervisor.

In either case, the supervisor should understand the kinds of child whom the service can help and the problems inherent in its use. It is desirable that the supervisor have experience and skill in working with children in their own family homes and in placement.

Use, method and amount of supervision may vary, but should carry out the purposes of supervision

- to assure the best possible service in behalf of each child, by the worker sharing responsibility with the supervisor
- as an administrative function, to appraise whether the worker meets the requirements and standards of performance of the agency

6.30   Staff development

The agency should provide an ongoing, carefully planned program of training for the development of the skills and knowledge of all staff.

Staff development should include

- supervision and inservice training
- staff meetings, seminars, consultation and other training devices
- regular evaluation of staff
- participation in professional meetings, conferences and workshops
- provision for an adequate professional library
- use of educational institutions for training and continuing education
- educational leaves, with scholarships or stipends for further training
- opportunities for staff to advance through experience into more responsible positions

Use of Supplementary Staff

Specialists such as psychiatrists and other mental health professionals, tutors, nutritionists, etc., should be available. In many communities, arrangements can be made with community resources. Consultation on nutrition is often available from state and local public health agencies.

6.31   Medical staff

The agency should employ one pediatrician or internist on a salary or fee basis to act as consultant to the agency in formulating and carrying out its policies for health and medical care.

The physician should be administratively responsible to the supervisor of the group home service for planning and supervising the health services and for coordinating them with the total program. A staff position is necessary even if the agency uses various medical, dental and other health services in the community.

Salaries or fees should be in accordance with prevailing fees in the community.

Any physician providing services, whether on salary or fee basis, should be regarded as a member of the staff responsible for the health program.

Appropriate medical specialists should be available for a group home caring for children with particular health needs, e.g., cystic fibrosis, cerebral palsy, etc.

6.32   Legal counsel

Legal counsel should be retained by the agency on a fee or salary basis.

Counsel services include
- clarifying any questionable legal status of a child under care
- interpreting to agency staff any provision of the laws governing agency operations, and their importance in daily child-placing practice and in the context of the large legal framework of foster care
- preparing appropriate legal papers and representing the agency on behalf of a child if this becomes necessary

It is inadvisable for the voluntary agency to use as its attorney a board member on a free or paid basis, or for the public agency to depend upon the state or county attorney general.

Changes in law in terms of the rights and responsibilities of child-placing agencies and the rights and responsibilities of parents and children will need continual scrutiny by an attorney to help the agency understand its position vis-a-vis the position of those it serves.

6.33 Volunteers

Volunteers may be used with some training and supervision to assist the staff of the group home and to enrich the program for the children with their special skills and talents.

Volunteers should not be used in place of paid staff.

The agency must respect the contributions volunteers can make, clearly define their responsibilities, and expect conscientious and regular attendance from them.

Volunteers can offer individual attention or they can bring to a group of children a special skill or talent.

Effective use of volunteers depends upon careful recruitment, selection, training and supervision.

Responsibility for the volunteer program should be assigned to a specific staff member.

6.34 Management and office staff

The agency should have a sufficient number of administrative and clerical staff members with qualifications for their respective responsibilities.

6.35 Workload of social workers

The number of families and children that can be adequately carried by a social worker should be determined by the agency, taking into account the various responsibilities assigned to a social worker in group home service.*

Units of work include intake, working with children in the group home, continual work with parents and other members of the family, collaboration with the group home staff and others serving the child and family.

It should be recognized that the group home staff and the social worker have to work together closely to assure consistency and continuity of the treatment plan.

Only one social worker should be assigned to each group home.

Personnel Practices and Policies

Every effort should be made to assure staff stability; frequent changes in personnel disrupt relationships and operations, and thus limit the capacity and effectiveness of the service.

6.36 Statement of personnel policies and practices

A written statement of personnel practices should be given to each staff member.

In public agencies, where personnel policies and practices are often determined by civil service commissions and legislatures, an advisory committee should be able to make recommendations for change when indicated.

Personnel policies and practices applicable to all staff should provide for
- job descriptions and qualifications for employment
- a defined time and method of evaluation
- employment benefits, including health insurances, retirement plan, social security and other insurances

---

*For children in foster family care, it has been estimated that a social service practitioner should provide service for no more than 20 to 30 children (see CWLA Standards for Foster Family Service 5.39). A social worker for a group home should provide service for no more than this number.

- hours of work, vacation, holidays, sick leave, leaves of absence
- channels for staff complaints and suggestions
- clarification of lines of authority

6.37 Personnel records

A personnel record should be kept for each staff member and should include date of beginning and end of employment, hours, salary or wages, qualifications, evaluations, resume and references. There should be a separate medical record, which the employee may have at termination of employment.

6.38 Salaries

Salaries should be established with ranges that provide for merit increases in each classification.

> To attract and retain adequate staff, salaries must be comparable to those paid by other agencies and organizations in the community for positions with similar qualifications and responsibilities. Periodic job analyses, development of job classifications and salary schedules should be used in all staff categories to facilitate competence.

6.39 Working Hours

Regularly scheduled hours of work should allow time for staff members to have sufficient relaxation from the demands of their assignment.

> Regular schedules for group home staff should include the equivalent of 2 days off in a planned work period.
>
> Group homes governed by wage and hour legislation should comply with the law. Other group homes should meet the same expectations.
>
> A weekly complement of four staff members would ordinarily assure both compliance with the law and essential care and

services for the care of the children in the group home. The heaviest concentration of staff should be when the children are in the home and in need of care and service. (5.2, 5.3)

6.40 Vacation

Vacation periods should conform to the practices of the community.

Staff, especially those who work closely or directly with the children, should have time off at planned intervals to maintain their strength, spirits and good humor.

Scheduling of vacations should be rotated to meet the needs of the service as well as the convenience of the staff members.

Office Facilities

6.41 Location and space

The office of the agency should be in a location accessible to children, their families and the group home, and should include comfortable offices with good lighting and ventilation, and separate interviewing rooms.

6.42 Case records

The agency should develop policies and guides for case recording for its staff.

Policies should include
- what information is sought and from whom
- what information is to be recorded and in what form
- who has access to case information and under what circumstances
- plans for retention and disposition of the records

Legal counsel familiar with the service should be involved in the development of the agency's record-keeping policy.

6.43 Record information

The agency should determine the information it needs about the children and families it serves and that which should be recorded.

The agency record should include
- child's name, age, race, religion, and legal status; names and addresses of parents and other family members
- reasons for the application, and source of referral
- periodic summaries of work with child and family, including current evaluation of the problem, the social service plan and goal

The record of the worker used by the supervisor for discussion of daily events and problems in work with the child and family is a time-limited tool and may not have to be retained.

6.44 Retention and disposition of case information

The agency should have a policy about what case information should be retained and for how long.

Some information will, of necessity, be retained: changes in the legal status of a child, and other situations where legal verifications may be required, or where an adult who was separated from his family during childhood may wish to learn about his early life.

6.45 Confidentiality

Every member of staff and every volunteer should be required to respect the privacy of the children and families and to act accordingly.

The agency's written policies should cover the many facets of confidentiality, including legislative and administrative regulations.

Staff members, volunteers, and bodies of governance should be fully informed of current agency policy and regulations protecting the privacy of the child and family.

The children and their families need to know about the policies and also about legislation, regulations and funding bodies that require disclosure of personal information. Ordinarily, any decision to release personal information requires the consent of the parent and/or the older child. Exceptions to this principle should be discussed with them so that they understand the conditions for using the service. Many issues concerning agency responsibility to provide confidentiality are under governmental and judicial review. As one aspect of its disclosure policy, the agency should evaluate any request for personal information, the likelihood of maintenance of confidentiality by a third party, and the pertinence of the requested information.

6.46   Use of statistics

The agency should keep a statistical record of the children and families who use group home service.

It should know the source of referral, kinds of problem, and the disposition of all applications.

Statistics should be kept for specific purposes. Staff should be informed by administration how the statistics they supply will be used.

Identification of children and families is not necessary in information needed by administration and board for internal use, such as volume of service given, appraisal of services, review in determination of policy and program planning, and interpretation of services given by the agency.

Responsibility for Community Participation

The agency providing child welfare services has a responsibility to identify unmet needs and to give leadership in stimulating improvement of the services. Group home service is one of a complex of services.

6.47 Purpose of interpretation

Both the board and staff should carry on an active program of interpretation and education within the community.

Interpretation is necessary to account to the community for the responsibility delegated to the agency, and to
- enlist the support of an informed citizenry essential for adequate financing and promotion of effective agency service
- encourage appropriate referrals for service from other community agencies and from key groups that often serve as sources of referral, such as health and mental health professionals and organizations, other social agencies, the court, and school personnel
- establish a basis for working with other professions to improve care and services for children

If a public relations consultant is employed, he or she should have a thorough understanding of agency programs.

6.48 Planning and coordination

The agency has a responsibility to join with other social agencies in the community to coordinate, plan and expand services for children and families who require them.

To ensure adequate and appropriate services for children and their families in accordance with their needs, and to prevent gaps in service resulting from restrictive eligibility requirements or from lack of resources, it is necessary to plan and sustain a coordinated program of both public and voluntary services for children and families.

Agency board and staff have a responsibility to constantly reassess and evaluate the agency's services so that its program may be adapted to the changing needs of the community.

The agency should participate in defining procedures for cooperative services and in developing more effective ways of integrating community services.

The agency should participate in projects to study and provide for children and families with particular social problems.

Special encouragement should be given to programs designed to provide for the social needs of children and families to conserve family life and prevent family breakdown. Such programs may be directed to the improvement of economic and social conditions that adversely affect children and the security of family life, as well as to the provision of necessary services in the community that strengthen families and offer help to them and their children.

7

COMMUNITY PLANNING AND ORGANIZATION FOR GROUP HOME SERVICE

A comprehensive planning program for child welfare services should be established in every community to provide a complete range of services under both public and voluntary auspices for children and their parents in a wide variety of situations. Such services will include some that have not yet been developed, as well as those currently existing. New patterns of community organization of services and of public-voluntary agency relationships may be required to enlist all relevant forces in the community in behalf of a particular child and family, on the basis of sound diagnosis and planning.

7.1 Responsibility for community planning

The state welfare department and a community planning body (such as the community council in urban communities, a citizens' committee on children and youth, and other organizations with social planning responsibilities) should be expected to provide leadership and resources.

They should assist in

- developing group home service for children, as well as other services that are lacking
- coordinating, improving and reorganizing existing services
- bringing about the participation of agencies, citizens and client groups in planning and coordinating services

The planning body must advocate adequate financing for group home service for children and must support efforts to make sufficient funds available through allocation of contributed funds and public appropriations.

Group home service for children may be provided under many different auspices but should be included among those services offered by public and voluntary child welfare agencies.

To ensure coverage, services of public and voluntary agencies should complement each other.

7.2   Planning for new group homes

The need for group homes should be given consideration in the planning of residential neighborhoods and in formulation or modification of zoning laws.

In planning for a new group home, members of the community should be consulted in selecting the site to minimize the risk of investing money and time on property in what may be or become an unsuitable location .

Zoning laws should provide the same regulations for group homes as for any family home, so that group homes can be available in sections where children generally reside.

7.3   Financing of voluntary agencies

Voluntary agencies providing group home service should be participating members of the community agency that distributes voluntary contributions for health and welfare services.

The board of the agency should be expected to raise funds for needed capital improvements, with the approval and support of the community planning agency. A voluntary agency, however, should not need to rely on its board alone to raise funds to meet basic operating expenses.

7.4   Use of public funds

Public support of group home service should be encouraged, in order to provide a necessary quality and quantity of service that may not be attainable through voluntary efforts.

The public agency responsible for child welfare services should make group home service available to children and their families on the basis of need alone, without regard to financial status, legal residence, social status, race or religion.

Public support may be given through allocation of operating funds, and purchase of care and service.

Public funds should be made available for construction, alteration and renovation as well as for operation of facilities.

Child Welfare Legislation

7.5 Legal regulation of group home service

Every state should legislate licensing of social agencies and community organizations that provide foster care for children, including group homes, regardless of the auspices of the agency.

State regulation of group home service is aimed primarily at the protection of children. When regulation is comprehensive, responsibly administered and carried out through well qualified staff with reasonable work assignments, local ordinances for protection of children in group homes may be unnecessary.

7.6 Responsibility of the state department that oversees or directly provides public child welfare services

The state department responsible for child welfare services should provide leadership in community planning and in the development of group home services so that they will be available to children in need of them.

The responsibilities of the state department should include

- development of standards and minimum requirements for licensing
- supervision of local public agencies in monitoring group home services
- establishment of an advisory committee on care of children, including group homes

• provision for a system of appeals and grievances, including a fair hearing under which applicants and recipients may appeal denial or exclusion from a service or failure to take into account their choice of service

• promotion of staff development and training programs to increase the availability of qualified professional and group home staff

• coordination and full use of existing services

• provision of group home services in all geographic areas for those who need them

• enlistment of participation of citizens and representatives of agencies and organizations in planning and developing adequate services

7.7 Information, reporting and statistics

The state department should bring together and coordinate all sources of information regarding available group home services, and the need for and availability of services throughout the state, and should disseminate such information to all communities.

7.8 Incorporation of facilities

The state department should give consultation and make recommendations concerning incorporation of group care facilities for children.

SELECTED REFERENCES

1. Bakal, Yitzhak. *Closing Correctional Institutions: New Strategies for Youth Services.* Lexington, Mass.: Lexington Books, 1973, 186 pp.
2. *Child Welfare League of America Standards for Foster Family Service,* Revised 1975. New York: CWLA, pp. 17-18.
3. *Child Welfare League of America Standards for Services of Child Welfare Institutions.* New York: CWLA, 1964, p.11.
4. Child Welfare League of America. *Group Homes in Perspective.* Eight papers reprinted from *Child Welfare.* New York: CWLA, 1964, 48 pp.
5. Costin, Lela B., editor. "Agency Group Homes," in *Child Welfare: Policies and Practice.* New York: McGraw-Hill, 1972, pp. 350-353.
6. Garber, Michael. "Neighborhood-Based Child Welfare," *Child Welfare,* LIV, 2 (February 1975) p. 73.
7. Greenberg, Arthur, and Mayer, Morris F. "Group Home Care as an Adjunct to Residential Treatment," *Child Welfare* LIV, 7 (July 1972).
8. Gula, Martin. "Community Services and Residential Institutions for Children," *Children Today,* III, 6 (November-December 1974) p. 15.
9. Gula, Martin. *Agency-Operated Group Homes: A Specialized Resource for Serving Children and Youth.* Washington, D.C. Children's Bureau, Welfare Administration, U.S. Department of Health, Education and Welfare, 1964, 35 pp.
10. Hirschbach, Ernest. "Memo to Child Care Workers on Their Role in Group Homes," *Child Welfare,* LV, 10 (December 1976), p. 681.
11. Hoffman, Linda R., et al. "A Group Home—Hospital Treatment Model for Severely Disturbed Adolescents," *Child Welfare,* LIV, 4 (April 1975), p. 283.
12. Jewett, Doris Rodman. "The Group Home: A Neighborhood-Based Treatment Facility," *Children Today,* II, 3 (May-June 1973), p. 16.
13. Lauber, Daniel, and Bangs, Frank S. *Zoning for Family and Group Care Facilities Report 300.* Chicago: American Society of Planning Officials, 1974, 30 pp.
14. Lawder, Elizabeth, et al. *Five Models of Foster Family Group Homes: A Systematic View of Foster Care.* New York: Child Welfare League of America, 1974. 97 pp.
15. Levine, Theodore. "Community-Based Treatment for Adolescents: Myths and Realities," *Social*

Work, XXII, 2 (March 1977), p. 144.
16. Maloney, Dennis M., et al. "BIABH Project: Regional Adaptation of the Teaching-Family Model Group Home for Adolescents," *Child Welfare*, LVI, 1 (January 1977) p. 787.
17. Mayer, Morris Fritz, et al. *Group Care of Children: Crossroads and Transitions.* New York: Child Welfare League of America, 1977, 327 pp.
18. National Association of Social Workers. *Encyclopedia of Social Work. 17th edition, Vol. I.* Washington, D.C. : NASW, 1977, pp. 131-134; 146-155.
19. Palmer, Ted. "The Youth Authority's Community Treatment Project," *Federal Probation* (March 1974), p.3.
20. Reid, Joseph H. "On Deinstitutionalization," *Child Welfare*, LIV, 4 (April 1975), p. 295.
21. Rohde, William L. "Urban Homes for Youths," *Social Work*, XX, 4 (July 1975), p. 324.
22. Schulman, Rena. "Examples of Adolescent Group Homes in Alliance With Larger Institutions." *Child Welfare*, LIV, 5 (May 1975), p. 341.
23. Stickney, Patricia, and Cupaiuolo, Anthony. "From CRISP: Strategies for Community Residences," *Child Welfare*, LV, 1 (January 1976), p. 54.
24. Taylor, Joseph L. "An Approach to the Treatment of Children in Group Residences, " *Journal of Communal Service*, LII, 3 (spring 1976), p. 286.
25. Taylor, Joseph L., et al. *A Group Home for Adolescent Girls: Practice and Research.* New York: CWLA 1976, 125 pp.

INDEX

A

Abridgment of parental rights, 2.15; laws for, 6.15
Administration, 6.11–6.48
Adolescents: for whom appropriate, 1.3; for whom not, 1.4; long-term care of, 1.5
Adoption, consideration of, 1.5
Advisory committee, 6.6, 6.10
Affiliations of agency, 6.48
Aftercare services, for child, 2.22
Agency: responsibility, 0.6, 1.7, 2.20; basis for continuing service, 2.10; and medical care, 2.16, 3.20–3.22; and foster parents, 2.19; intake procedure 3.16; and education, 3.28; qualifications and prerequisites, 6.0; different kinds of service in, 6.1; legal qualifications for, 6.2–6.5; policies of, 6.11; evaluation of services, 6.12; and legal responsibility, 6.14; budget, 6.16; financial support for, 6.17; planning, 6.48
Agency services: need for, 0.1–0.2; costs of, 6.18
Agreements between parents and agency, 2.20
Allowances, 3.2
Appeals, procedures for, 6.13, 7.6
Appropriate care, selection of, 0.6
Assumption of legal responsibility for child, 6.2–6.5; 6.14
Auspices of service, 6.1
Authorization of agency, 6.2

B

Basic physical conditions for selection of group homes, 4.7, 4.8
Basic principles, 0.2
Board of directors: composition of, 6.6; qualifications of, 6.7; change of membership, 6.8; responsibilities of, 6.9
Budget, 6.16

C

Care of child, 0.6, 1.6–1.7; duration of, 1–5, 2.1, 2.11–2.12, 2.20; provisions for, 2.2–2.6; costs of, 6.19–6.21; aftercare, 2.22
Case loads, 6.35
Case planning, 2.13, 2.14, 3.18
Case records, 6.42–6.44
Changing patterns of child care, 0.1, 0.2
Characteristics: of children in group homes, 0.3, 1.3; of families, 2.1
Child: services for, 2.9, 2.10, 2.12; planning and evaluation of treatment, 2.13
Children: responsibility for, 0.1; for whom group home service is appropriate, 1.3; for whom group home service is not appropriate, 1.4; parents' right to visit, 2.19; number of, in group home, 3.12; with school problems, 3.30; legal status of, 6.15
Coed living, in group home, 3.14
Clothing, 3.1
College education, 3.28, 3.32
Community: relations with, 4.1; selection of, 4.2, 4.7; response to concerns of, 4.3; zoning as a factor, 4.5; as source of recruitment of staff, 5.7; participation of, 6.47, 6.48; as source of financing, 7.3, 7.4
Community planning: responsibility for, 7.1, 7.6; new group homes, 7.2
Components of group home service, 0.4, 1.1, 1.2
Composition of group home, 3.13

81

Confidentiality, 6.45
Consultants, qualifications and use of, 6.31, 6.32
Cost components, for child using group home service, 6.19–6.21
Costs, reimbursement of, 6.17, 6.20
Counsel, legal, 6.32
Court, referrals by, 2.4
Custody, *see* Legal custody

D

Decision to use service, 1.3
Definition of group home care, 1.1, 1.2
Delegation of parental responsibilities, 2.11, 2.15
Dental care, 3.25
Determination: of legal responsibility and legal status, 6.14, 6.15; of religious affiliation, 2.15, 2.18
Development of group homes, 4.1–4.7
Direct social services of state department, 7.6–7.8
Director, group home service, 6.9, 6.22
Duration of services, 1.5

E

Education, 3.28–3.30; higher, 3.32
Emergency care in illness, 2.16, 3.22, 3.24, 3.25
Emergency group home, 1.3
Emotional problems, children with, 1.3, 1.4, 1.5. 2.1, 2.6, 3.26
Employment of married couple, 5.3
Enhancement of parental functioning, 1.6, 2.1, 2.11, 2.17, 2.19, 2.21, 2.22, 3.18, 3.19
Evaluation: of plan, 2.13; of service, 3.15, 3.18, 6.12

F

Facilities: neighborhood, 4.7; home, 4.8–4.16, 4.18; staff, 4.17; office, 6.41
Family group home, 0.2, 4.18

Financing, 6.16, 6.17, 7.3, 7.4
Foster parents, 2.19
Frequency of interviews, 2.7, 2.10–2.12, 2.20

G

Goals, setting, 2.9
Grievance procedures, 2.4
Group composition, 3.13
Group home staff: living accommodations for, 4.17; size, 6.23; qualifications of, 6.26; physical examinations of, 6.27; supervision of, 6.24
Group home: raison d'etre, 0.2, 0.3; house rules, 3.4; milieu of, 3.1; responsibilities of child in, 3.2–3.4; rules in, 3.4, 3.5; staff, adult model, 3.6; recreation, 3.11; number of children in, 3.12; coeducation, 3.14; care of sick child, 3.23; and health services, 3.22–3.25; recreational activities, 3.33; relationship with the community, 4.1, 4.3; environment of, 4.1–4.4; considerations in choice of, 4.5, 4.7; rent or buy?, 4.6; daily living in, 4.8–4.14; layout of, 4.8–4.14; furnishings and equipment, 4.15, 4.16; maintenance, 4.19; safety and sanitation, 4.20; administrative structure, 6.22; administrative responsibility for, 6.24; supervisor of group home staff, 6.25; planning for, 7.2
Group home service: bases of, 0.2; characteristics of, 0.4, 0.5, 1.1; goals, 1.2, 2.9; for whom?, 1.3; duration, 1.5; termination, 2.21; intake, 3.15; planning and evaluating, 3.18; relationship with school personnel, 3.29; community planning for, 7.1, 7.2; financing, 7.3; frequency of interviews, 2.1, 2.7, 2.10, 2.11, 2.12, 2.20

Group interaction, 3.7–3.8
Group meetings, 3.9–3.10
Guardianship or legal custody, 6.15

H

Health: records, 3.25; services, 3.20–3.23
Help to parents, 1.6, 2.1, 2.11, 2.19
Hospitalization, 3.24

I

Incorporation of voluntary agency, 6.3
Intake study, 1.6, 2.7
Integration of services, 5.4
Interagency cooperation, 2.2
Interpretation, to community, 6.47

L

Legal counsel, 6.32
Legal custody, 2.15, 6.15; transfer of, 2.15
Legal responsibility for child, assumption of, 2.20, 6.14
Legal rights of parents, 2.15–2.20
Legal status, of child, 6.15, 6.32
Legislation, regulation for licensing, 7.5
Licensing, of group homes, 6.5
Limitation of parental rights, 2.15

M

Management of visits, 2.19
Married couples, as staff, 4.17, 5.3
Medical care, responsibility for, 2.16
Medical staff, 6.31
Mental health services, 3.26

N

Need: for agency services, 0.2, 0.3; for social work, 2.1; for intake study, 2.7
Number of children, in group home, 3.12

O

Objectives of group home care, 0.4, 1.2
Office: staff, 6.34; facilities, 6.41

P

Parents: service to, 1.6; problems of, 2.1; help from social worker, 2.11; rights and responsibilities, 2.15–2.20; role in placement of child, 3.17
Participation in planning: by children, 1.1, 1.6, 2.9, 2.14; by staff, 1.1, 2.12, 2.13; by parents, 1.6, 2.4, 2.9; by social workers, 2.1, 2.9, 2.13; by state department, 7.6; by community, 4.3, 7.2; by agency, 4.1–4.3, 6.48
Payment: by other agencies, 2.2; by parents, 2.10, 2.17, 2.20
Periodic review: of service, 0.6, 1.6, 3.18, 6.9, 6.12; of children in service, 3.18; of staff, 6.30
Personnel practices and policies, 6.36–6.40
Personnel records, 6.37
Physician, 3.21, 6.31
Placement, introduction to, 3.17
Placement on court order, 2.20
Planning, *see* Participation in planning
Policies: formulation of, 6.9, 6.11; personnel, 6.36–6.40
Psychiatric services, 3.26
Psychologist, 3.27

Q

Qualifications: for board or advisory committee membership, 6.7; of supervisor of group home staff, 6.25; of group home staff, 6.26; of social workers, 6.28

R

Reasons for placement, 1.3
Records, case, 6.42–6.44

Recreation, 4.10
Recreational activities, 3.33, 3.34
Referrals, 2.3–2.6, 2.8, 2.11
Religion, 2.15, 2.18
Rights of children, 0.2

S

Salaries, 6.38
School attendance, 3.28–3.30
Sleeping arrangements, 4.12
Social work, 2.1
Social worker: help to parents, 2.11; and child, 2.12; responsibilities of, 2.13; and aftercare, 2.22; in group meetings, 3.10; participation in intake decision, 3.15, 3.16; role in planning and evaluating use of service, 3.18; and school personnel, 3.29; in group home service, 6.28; supervision of, 6.29; workload of, 6.35
Special interests, development of, 3.31
Staff, group home: 5.1, 5.2; working hours, 5.3, 6.39; other personnel, 5.5; responsibilities of, 5.6; recruitment of, 5.7; supervision of, 5.8; size of, 6.23, 6.39
Staff, social work: qualifications of, 6.28; supervision of, 6.29; development of, 6.30; workloads of, 6.35; size of staff, 6.23
State department responsibilities for child welfare services, 7.6–7.8
Statistics, use of, 6.46
Supervision of group home staff, 5.8
Supervisor: social work, 6.22, 6.29; group home staff, 6.25, 6.29
Supplementary staff, qualifications and use of, 5.5; kinds and duties, 6.31–6.33

T

Television, use of, 3.33
Termination of parental rights, 2.15
Termination of service, 3.19, 3.21

V

Vocational counseling and training, 3.32
Volunteers, 6.33

W

Workload, social workers, 6.35
Written agreement, 2.20